COACHING
101
a Simplified Guide to Being a
Great Coach in Business

COACHING
101
a Simplified Guide to Being a
Great Coach in Business

NANCY DEWAR

COACHING 101 A SIMPLIFIED GUIDE TO BEING A GREAT COACH IN BUSINESS

The views expressed in this work are solely those of the author and do not necessarily reflect the views of the publisher, and the publisher hereby disclaims any responsibility for them.

iUniverse books may be ordered through booksellers or by contacting:

iUniverse
1663 Liberty Drive
Bloomington, IN 47403
www.iuniverse.com
1-800-Authors (1-800-288-4677)

Because of the dynamic nature of the Internet, any web addresses or links contained in this book may have changed since publication and may no longer be valid. The views expressed in this work are solely those of the author and do not necessarily reflect the views of the publisher, and the publisher hereby disclaims any responsibility for them.

Any people depicted in stock imagery provided by Getty Images are models, and such images are being used for illustrative purposes only. Certain stock imagery © Getty Images.

ISBN: 978-1-5320-6047-2 (sc)
ISBN: 978-1-5320-6048-9 (e)

Library of Congress Control Number: 2018912293

Print information available on the last page.

iUniverse rev. date: 10/24/2018

Contents

Opening

THE TERM *COACHING* IS being used in many ways and has become a bit of a trend. For those of us who are certified coaches, it causes a bit of an angst. The profession of coaching has worked very hard to create a code of ethics and standards to ensure the credibility and consistency of the skill is being delivered. For many years, I shied away from calling myself a coach because it was perceived as fluffy or soft. But then I realized that everything I had done in my career was coaching, and the many times I had helped develop people's careers and improve their skills was actually a talent—something to be proud of, not ashamed. I decided to get my coaching credentials so that I could then use this skill in a credible way, I used my background in business. Business coaching is not soft; it is transformative. When you have the right chemistry with the right coach fit, it will help anyone get to the next level. Every great athlete and every successful team has at least one thing in common: a great coach! So why, when it comes to business, do many think a coach is not needed or effective?

I wanted to write this book for two reasons. The first was to dispel the myth about what coaching is, and the second was to make it easier for coaching to become a new way for people to talk to each other and help each other in the workplace. When I work with organizations and teach them how to coach, the first hurdle is to have leaders stop directing and start asking. It is amazing the difference in a conversation when we start with opening up the dialogue with a question versus going in with our own agendas. Oh, what we learn!

The second thing I notice with leaders is that they think coaching happens twice a year at performance development conversations, when they talk about their employees' careers and next steps. This is where the dynamic needs to change in order to creating a coaching culture where the conversations are always started with a question versus an ask. Creating this kind of dynamic in an organization changes the way employees feel about their bosses; their engagement is higher, and the results follow.

I am not immune to this. As a leader, I have an agenda, and I know how hard it is to pull back when all I want to do is tell them what to do. But I know I have hired smart, capable people who can figure it out and who have great ideas of their own. So I ask, not tell, and that has been my mantra since I started doing this coaching thing, even before I knew it was a profession.

My goal is to make this easy for you as a leader to coach and be successful. You will understand what it is, and you'll have a pocket guide to help you get better at it. Your people will love you for it, and in return your organization will have motivated, engaged employees thriving in their roles and producing the best results. Many people ask me if there is an ROI for coaching, and there is; we have done the math. But the real test is in how your employees feel. Simply ask them!

What Is Coaching?

COACHING IS PARTNERING WITH clients in a thought-provoking and creative process that inspires clients to maximize their personal and professional potential. It involves unlocking people's potential to maximize their growth. It is an ongoing process that uncovers, develops, and helps actualize potential while enhancing performance through commitment and accountability.

The goal of coaching is to draw out the underlying issues or causes and help people to better understand for themselves what is going on. With that information, they can then determine where they would like to go and any changes they want to make. A coach will help them build a plan to move in a different direction.

A coach helps people tap into the unconscious mind—the largest and most powerful part of the mind that holds all awareness that is not presently in the conscious mind. All memories, feelings, and thoughts that are out of conscious awareness are by definition unconscious. It is also called the subconscious and is known as the dreaming mind or the deep mind.

Coaching focuses on people's specific challenges, helping them get unstuck and move forward, rather than general career development or personal problems. The key is in the approach: a coach relies on the coachees to find their own answers rather than showing or telling them what to do. Coaches do this by asking the right questions to help the coachees discover what they already know.

Coaching is:

- Asking powerful questions that will allow people to find their own solutions.
- Supporting the person being coached to find proper people and resources.
- Fostering individual performance while focusing on future and professional development.
- Creating solutions that result in sustained change.

Coaching versus Consulting, Mentoring, and Counseling

Coaching is often confused with other types of business methodologies. The attached chart helps to better understand the difference in focus and direction. In business we are often asked to do a combination of coaching and mentoring with our teams. We have to be prepared to wear different hats at different times. The main goal is to start every conversation with a coach approach and then move to mentoring when appropriate.

"A coach is someone who tells you what you don't want to hear, who has you see what you don't want to see, so you can be who you always known you could be."

—Tom Landry

	Coaching	Consulting	Mentoring	Counselling
Focus	Specific challenges, helping you get unstuck, moving forward	Organizational issues	Career Development	Personal/ emotional problems or performance issues
Approach	Not telling someone what to do, relying on clients for finding their own answers	Assessing the needs and making a recommendation	Having a more-experienced colleague guide a protégé	Correcting dysfunctional thinking and behaviours
Process	Asking the right questions to help clients discover what they already know	Relies on experience to guide, rather than promote self-discovery	Obtains career goals; guides them for a career choice or career move	Explore and analyze deep-rooted behavior or emotions
Structure	Usually a defined time commitment; has an action plan	Comes in for a specific period of time and for a specific need	Often informal; longer-term career development	Often a long process where you may be looking at neuroses
Source of information	Based on objective facts that are data based (assessments)	Works from results-oriented contract with client	Experience-driven conversations	Uses professional guidelines to identify and analyze the root of the problem

2

The Benefits of Coaching

PROFESSIONAL COACHING BRINGS MANY wonderful benefits.

- ❖ Fresh perspectives on personal challenges
- ❖ Enhanced decision-making skills
- ❖ Greater interpersonal effectiveness
- ❖ Increased confidence
- ❖ Appreciable improvement in productivity
- ❖ Greater satisfaction with life and work
- ❖ Attainment of relevant goals
- ❖ Someone to bounce ideas off of

Improved Work Performance	Improved Business Management	Improved Time Management	Improved Team Effectiveness
70%	61%	57%	51%

Source: ICF Global Coaching Client Study was commissioned by the ICF but conducted independently by PricewaterhouseCoopers.

Iceberg Analogy for Coaching

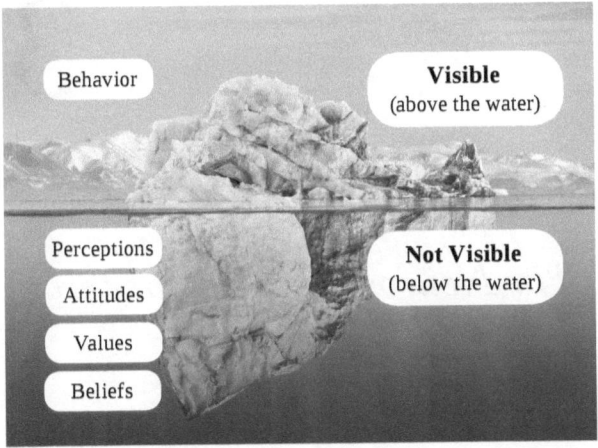

An iceberg can serve as a useful metaphor to understand the unconscious mind, its relationship to the conscious mind, and how the two parts of our mind can better work together. As an iceberg floats in the water, the huge mass of it remains below the surface.

The conscious mind is what we notice above the surface. The unconscious mind, the largest and most powerful part, remains unseen below the surface.

The unconscious mind holds all awareness that is not presently in the conscious mind. All memories, feelings, and thoughts that are out of conscious awareness are by definition unconscious. It is also called the subconscious and is known as the dreaming mind or the deep mind.

Coaching's goal is to draw out the underlying issues or causes and help people to better understand for themselves what is going on. Then you can determine where they would like to go and any changes they want to make. A coach then will help them build a plan to move in a different direction

3

The Neuroscience of Coaching

COACHES GAIN A SENSE of credibility when they can explain the research that backs up what they are doing with the people they are coaching.

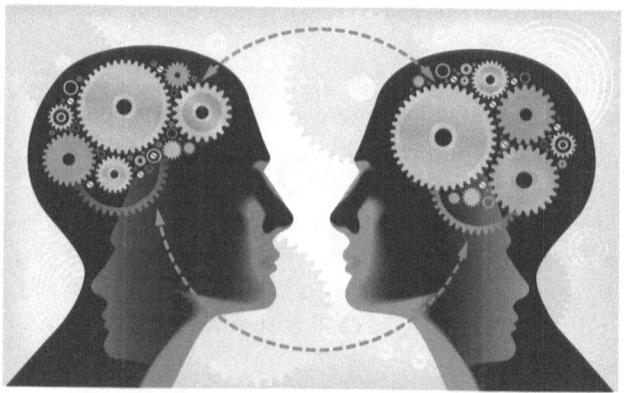

People's ability to take in information, think, and then act is precious. Coaching has the potential to not only help the person you are working with improve in these skills but also have a positive ripple effect.

If you are going to be working with people's minds and brains, then it is logical to know as much as you can about how these things actually work.

We are equipped to understand what is going on in the brain through the field of neuroscience, and so we need to continue to be discerning in how we select our coaches. We want the best, most qualified, and most reliable people.

Good and experienced coaches know that there is a lot more to coaching than simply doing exercise after exercise with a client. This is where neuroscience comes in.

Neuroscience for Coaches Insights e-Book: https://www.slideshare.net/AmyBrann/neuroscience-for-coaches-insights-ebook

We have 3 functioning brains:

Head	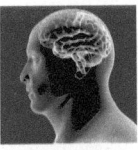	***Observing the world*** creativity; continuously generating new ideas; living authentically as who you are; knowing that you have the power of choice; inner life of logic, reasoning, detailed, future, and plans
Heart		***Reaching out to the World*** compassion; encompasses love as well as a manner of relating to yourself and to others; a loving kindness; inner life of emotions, memories, images, visions, and dreams
Gut	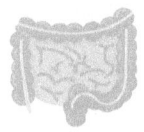	***Directly Engaged with the World*** courage; physiologically maintain your sense of core identity; keep you safe from harm (fight or flight); taking action; mobilization; instinct and intuition; unselfconscious, immediate, practical, and direct

Wisdom comes when the three brains are working together, aligned and integrated. Wisdom is an emergent quality that is the result of harnessing the perspectives and insights from all the brains when they are functioning at their highest level of intelligence.

Increase Your Brain Power! Use All 3 Brains (http://melissaalexisjacobsen. com/increase-your-brain-power-use-all-3-brains/)

The three brains do different things.

- Head brain: cognitive perception, thinking, making meaning
- Gut brain: identity, self-preservation, mobilization
- Heart brain: emoting, values, relationship effects

Thinking, memory storage, responsiveness, and intelligence are not limited to our heads but are also in our hearts and guts.

By understanding the complexities and how the three brains work together, we offer valuable insight to coaching because we are able to explore people's issues further while deciphering how we need to coach to each of the brains.

Being able to access all three brains allow us to help those people being coached to make important decisions and to get them aligned to their business challenges. All three need to be come into play, be integrated, and be harnessed to their highest potential when it comes to any decision-making process.

If the heart is not integrated, two things emerge.

1. People may or may not connect to the strategy, which may decrease staff engagement and change organizational culture.
2. Burnout: push for numbers and work hard without the sense of feeling valued and fulfilled.

When all three brains are integrated, we can inspire, coach, and make a difference.

It has to start with a heart-based connection of wanting to add value and do good. Coaching to the heart really shows people that doing good and appreciating people is good for business. Effectively coaching and connecting the real human values leads to finding inspiration and passion when engagement is no longer a problem, because people will stay connected to work that is meaningful.

When the heart is compassionately connected to what's happening, then the head and gut become connected and creative.

The latest advances in neuroscience findings for workplace coaching: https://www.youtube.com/watch?v=E0Hh2eT-ulE

Understanding People

		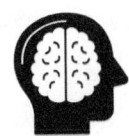	
The results your organization achieves are at least partly dependent on your people.	If you understand people better, you can improve behaviors and therefore results.	Neuroscience helps us understand people.	Leads to enhanced performance—Adventures with Agile.

Neuroscience for Coaches (Performance and Innovation) with Amy Brann (https://www.eventbrite.co.uk/e/neuroscience-for-coaches-performance-and-innovation-with-amy-brann-registration-36748938063)

4

Why Do We Do Coaching in Business?

GOOD COMPANIES BELIEVE IN supporting and developing their people so that they can create opportunities to promote from within. Coaching enables a culture of development and support that ensures people are given the proper tools for their own personal goals while meeting the needs of the company.

The coaching approach that you will create will feel different for employees. They will feel empowered to make decisions and self-discover areas of opportunity for themselves and their business units. Studies show that organizations that do coaching retain the best talent and have engaged and loyal employees. We know that engaged employees lead to engaged customers, and so the business model for coaching is easy to understand.

The skills and competencies of a good coach can also be leveraged no matter what role you are in. Using good listening skills, being present, and asking versus telling are all good strategies for building strong relationships and getting results.

Coaching is here to stay, and any organization that wants to compete with the most empowered and productive teams will use it as a way to ensure it is growing its teams and meeting the needs of its customers.

5

Your Role as a Coach

EACH ROLE WILL HAVE some unique aspects of how to coach. However, the basics of coaching—ask, don't tell, and letting others self-discover—will be the same no matter what role you are in.

Some of you will be coaching in the field more regularly and will be able to do more face-to-face coaching sessions. If you are not office-based or in a role where your employees are remote, you may need to use different forums for coaching, like virtual or Skype, and the number of touch points may not be as frequent.

Either way, you are encouraged to always plan some time for coaching in your regular one-on-ones so that you are doing it as often as possible. A coaching approach should be used with any conversation because it opens up the employee in a completely different way and allows for greater trust and alignment in the next steps.

If you are unsure of when and where to coach, you should have this conversation with your manager to help you build in the time for coaching.

6

Creating a Coaching Culture

A COACHING CULTURE IS built on organizational and leadership beliefs and practices that reflect coaching as a strategic business driver and an essential talent-management tool. A coaching culture creates a common coaching language and process, and it builds shared belief in and commitment to the value of coaching. A coaching culture embraces and maximizes individual and team strengths to drive business outcomes, which leads to increased productivity, more successful change initiatives, and greater field execution success.

If, as leaders and managers, we have done our due diligence in hiring and supporting the right people, then why would we not always ensure they are motivated and are thriving? Companies spend millions of dollars on hiring and onboarding new employees but forget that retaining the ones they already have is a better overall strategy and is cheaper.

A company's overall culture or philosophy on employee engagement and development will help to retain and grow the best talent. A culture of coaching will create the most loyal employees and produce the best results. Understanding how to create leaders who know how to develop is also a challenge for some organizations. Sometimes those who can sell the most business or are the most extroverted are the ones getting promoted, but the real heroes are the ones who know how to support and work with teams of people to develop them to the next level and achieve outstanding results. Unfortunately, these unsung heroes don't get the recognition or support they deserve, despite often being the reason other employees stay.

With a coaching mindset, you look through the lens of opportunity, not resistance. You determine the why behind behaviors, and as a leader you adjust your own behavior to produce the results you need. You have to believe that people are genuinely good and want to be seen as capable. People generally want to add value and feel like they are contributing. How, as a leader, are you opening the doors for your employees to achieve their goals?

Creating clarity for people on how they can make an impact to the overall goals will help them to feel motivated and focused. By using a strengths-based approach, understanding what they naturally are good at and where they can contribute most, and setting them up for success, you will align the person and the business to move forward in the same direction. That is our role as leaders and coaches.

An organization with a coaching mindset is not about fluffy, soft conversations; it is about creating a great place to work and developing your people and your business to create the best outcomes for both. As a leader, you do not have to feel like a coach mindset is difficult. Simply be genuine and treat employees like they were your kids or family members, and you truly care for and only the want best for them. That is the shift in mindset that will help change the way employees feel about you as a leader, and the rewards (both personally and professionally) will be many.

What does it feel like to work in your organization? Are you excited and motivated to be a part of your workplace? Do you feel optimistic that when things go wrong or mistakes are made, situations will be handled in a trusting and respectful way?

As coaches, we say that we like to handle things with a coach approach. It is a mindset shift that takes away the old way of thinking that managers know all and should be heavy-handed in their approach. It replaces it with an approach that allows for co-workers to discover the basis of any issue with a lens of trust and support versus assuming bad faith or placing blame. It is the approach that says we are in this together and will figure it out, versus looking for the scapegoat.

As leaders and managers, if we have done our due diligence in hiring and supporting the right people, then why would we not always ensure they are motivated and are thriving? Companies spend millions of dollars on hiring and onboarding new employees and forget that retaining the ones we have is a better overall strategy and cheaper.

A company's overall culture or philosophy on employee engagement and development will help to retain and grow the best talent. A culture of coaching will create the most loyal employees and produce the best results. Understanding how to create leaders who know how to develop is also a challenge for some organizations. Sometimes those who can sell the most business or are the most extroverted are the ones getting promoted. The real heroes are the ones who know how to support and work with teams of people to develop them to the next level and achieve outstanding results. Unfortunately, these unsung heroes don't get the recognition or support they deserve, but they are often the reason others employees stay.

With a coaching mindset, you look through the lens of opportunity, not resistance. You determine the why behind behaviors and as leaders adjust your own behavior to produce the results you need.

You have to believe that people are genuinely good and want to be seen as capable. People generally want to add value and feel like they are contributing, so as a leader, how are you opening the doors for your employees to achieve their goals?

I have worked in organizations that have the coach approach and some that didn't. When I look back at my career, I can see how I grew and flourished in the ones that did. My mindset and approach has been shaped by those great leaders who had the vision and the philosophy to care for me as person and make me feel like my contribution was worthy. They took the time to ask the questions of clarity to fully understand and used words like "I trust you and know you will make it happen." This is empowering people to be at their best, and what we get back as employers is tenfold. You get much more than what is in any job description. You create a sense of team, dedication, and commitment to the business goals while working through each person's personal journey.

Creating clarity for people regarding how they can make an impact to the overall goals will help them to feel motivated and focused. By using a strengths-based approach, understanding what they naturally are good at and where they can contribute most, and setting them up for success, you will align the person and the business to move forward in the same direction. That is our role as leaders and coaches

An organization with a coaching mindset is not about fluffy, soft conversations' it is about creating a great place to work and developing your people and your business to create the best outcomes for both. As leaders, you do not have to feel like a coach mindset is difficult. Simply be genuine and treat employees like they were your kids or family members, and you truly care for and only the want best for them. That is the shift in mindset that will help change the way employees feel about you as a leader and the rewards (both personally and professionally) will be many.

7

Coaching Competencies

COACHING COMPETENCIES SUPPORT A coach's understanding about the skills and approaches used when coaching. They help to define our role as a coach, are our gold standard that we work toward as coaches and measure our skill set against. We are always working toward these. No coach starts as a master of these competencies, but good coaches are always working toward improving their skill set and measuring themselves against these ideals. Not only do these competencies define what you do, but you can also use them to help you through difficult coaching conversations, helping you to remember how to best approach a situation.

The following eight coaching competencies were developed in accordance with the International Coach Federation to help coaches better understand the approaches that will help them promote successful coaching partnerships.

Coaching Competencies

1. Coach with the use of listening skills to dig for the root cause of issues.
2. Enable self-discovery with an appreciative coaching approach based on strengths.
3. Self-reflect on and continue to grow both your own performance and that of your team's; identify gaps and opportunity areas.
4. Be open to new and different approaches and embrace and lead change.
5. Use a balanced approach to coaching, mentor, and coach.
6. Use powerful questions and probing techniques—ask, don't tell. — *Ask not Tell*
7. Be fully present.
8. Be able to give and take feedback with a coach approach.

8

Coaching as a Mindset

WORKING WITH INDIVIDUALS AND organizations to understand and utilize a coaching mindset requires a full transition in how we think. Typically, when we talk about corporate coaching, we think of a structured session where we sit with a coach, address specific objectives, and follow a structured process.

Leaders often ask, "So when do I start the coaching, and how long do I make the session?" My response is that this is not a set agenda item. It should not be "Let's set twenty minutes to coach and then move on to our other business items."

Every conversation, every interaction with a team, should be with a coach approach. This is a shift in philosophy to an "ask, not tell" mindset. Although it sounds simple, it is not easy.

As leaders, we are taught that we should have the answers and be the ones providing direction. But the truth is the power of leadership is understanding how to draw out the ideas from your team. True credibility comes from listening to all perspectives and choosing the ones that make sense based on the business need. We are not always the closest to the day to day issues, and if we trust and respect our team, then hearing their ideas and perspectives should be the guiding force to help us in making our decisions. In the process, we engage and build credibility with our team at a whole new level.

Some leaders may not be comfortable with this approach because they may feel a loss of control. Getting used to releasing your power to the team is the key to unlocking the potential of the ideas and moving the business forward in new directions.

How do we teach an "ask, not tell" mindset? It's an approach that can be successful in all facets of your life. Think about how you may disarm a potentially controversial topic with anyone if you approach it with a question versus a directive. Your kids, your friends, or your partner will naturally be less defensive, and the depth and richness of the conversation can reach a whole new level. It says "I trust you and respect your ideas" versus "I know all, and you know nothing, so I have to tell you." Anyone who has teenage kids may relate to this. Teenagers want to feel like they have control in their lives, but they still need a lot of direction. How we approach these conversations can open up a deeper understanding of what they are thinking, and it can help us to better understand the why. Any decision that is made collaboratively versus force automatically breeds stronger engagement. It takes some of the pressure off of you, as a leader, to always come up with the ideas or the resolution. It also trains your team to make decisions, which can be a strategy to grow talent from within.

It sometimes is as simple as stopping yourself the next time you are starting to communicate a directive. Instead, use some open-ended questions that start with understanding what don't you know that you should. Great leaders are great listeners, and they are constantly curious about this question: "What do I need to know that I don't?" The more you use this approach in all facets of your life, the more of a habit it will become. The mindset shift is powerful, and the results may surprise you

9

Strengths Based Coaching

Strengths-Based Approach

A STRENGTHS-BASED APPROACH TO coaching focuses on enhancing a person's *strengths* rather than one's weaknesses. This type of coaching is believed to contribute to higher levels of positivity, greater engagement, and sustained peak performance.

This approach to coaching is built on the understanding that people already have the answers for how to be their very best selves, and when you help them self-discover these answers by understanding their strengths, they will be better positioned to deliver successful outcomes.

Strengths-based coaching encourages people to use their strengths to manage any opportunities that could lead to performance risk, and to utilize their strengths to bring them even greater success in the workplace.

Focusing on strengths makes it easier to accomplish goals set during a coaching session because it leverages what we know and energizes us. It can also help individuals focus on the positive and lean on their strengths to overcome barriers. We use the basis of appreciative inquiry to help us in coaching.

> "We can't ignore problems—we just need to approach them from the other side." — Cooperrider and Whitney, 2001

The Four Stages of Appreciative Inquiry

There are four stages involved in appreciative inquiry: discovery, dream, design, and destiny/delivery. The completion of these stages result in "transformational change, sourced from collaborative inquiry with participants" (Clancy 2007). Let's take a closer look at the four stages.

1. Discovery

Whatever the situation at hand, the first step is to "discover and disclose [its] positive capacity" (Cooperrider and Whitney 2001). The discovery stage aims to find, emphasize, and illuminate any factors that have led to "the best" in a given situation (Ludema, Cooperrider, and Barrett 2001).

When discovering the best, you can start by looking at the peak experiences. However, it is equally important to pay attention to that which is surprising, that which touches your heart and spirit, and that which forces you to look differently at reality (Bushe 2007).

In general, most of the process of the discovery stage is about "eliciting a positive discourse (e.g., stories, **examples**, metaphors) about organizational, family or community life" (Cram 2010).

In an organizational setting, possible positive discovery questions could be:

- What gives life to our organization and allows it to function at its best?
- What in this particular setting or context makes organizing possible? (Ludema, Cooperrider, and Barrett 2001)

Examples of questions for your daily life could be:

- What are the most significant stories in my life?
- Where are things going well in my life?
- Where am I making a difference? (Cram 2010)

2. Dream

"Uncover values and aspirations [you] might not have been aware of" (Bushe 2007).

Once you have discovered the best, there comes the dream stage.

This is where you begin to dream of what could be or needs to be. Basically, the dream stage challenges the status quo and works on the blue sky potential (Cram 2010).

In the dream stage, you focus on the possibility of what could be rather than on the limiting ways people normally do, feel, see, act, or react, and through this you will begin to see and understand things in a new way.

Froman (2010) offers an example of the dream stage where participants work together to come up with a representation of their highest aspirations and dreams for their ideal future. These representations could be in art, poetry, or acting (Froman 2010).

Furthermore, rather than creating a mission statement, the dream stage "results in something more symbolic, like a graphical representation" (Bushe 2011).

3. Design

The next step in the process is the design stage. It is time for creating or designing what you want and looking at how your ideal scenario could work. Generally, the design stage is "a process of finding common ground by sharing discoveries and possibilities, dialoguing and debating" (Ludema, Cooperrider, and Barrett 2001), which gets you to the point where people agree on how they are going to make it happen.

In the design stage, the group has to "identify concrete, actionable ideas that will move the organization closer to its newly envisioned potential" (Froman 2010).

4. Destiny

The last *D* stands for destiny, which is defined as "an invitation to construct the future through innovation and action" (Ludema, Cooperrider, and Barrett 2001).

The destiny stage is when people commit to the aspirations they want to achieve (Cram 2010).

During this stage, the implementation of change is emphasized. The "most obvious effects are found in the degree to which teams carry out their plans" (Froman 2010).

Appreciative Inquiry and Positive Psychology

Appreciative inquiry indirectly collaborates with positive psychology with its strengths-based approach (Boyd and Bright 2007). Furthermore, appreciative inquiry can also "increase positive feelings, the positive talk ratio, and make generative thinking and acting more likely" (Bushe 2007).

Similar to strengths in positive psychology, appreciative inquiry focuses on what's already working inside your family, organization, or community. In this way, it can "describe a preferred future for the organisation alongside an understanding of how an organisation can build toward that future" (Cram 2010).

Moreover, appreciative inquiry recognizes people not by role but by relationship, which gives the opportunity for people to raise their voices and be heard (Whitney and Trosten-Bloom 2010).

In conclusion, appreciative inquiry can teach you to approach a situation with a new perspective that considers all possible aspects with a positive, strengths-based focus. Appreciative inquiry offers all of us the opportunity to broaden our perspectives and create positive outcomes.

10

Overcoming the Resistance to Coaching

GAINING BUY-IN ON COACHING with an individual who may not have asked for coaching is not easy. Employees may be told they need a coach from a performance management standpoint, or their organization may be focusing on coaching as a management skill development area. Either way, resistance can hold back the process and deter great results.

Gaining buy-in can be a slow road and usually is a combination of factors. First, the right coach fit is imperative for people to see the credibility. There needs to be the right chemistry and business acumen so that the coach can relate to the coachees' world. Finding the right coach is like hiring an employee: you don't simply hire the first person who applied; you review credentials and have a test session to understand fit. Good coaches will take the time to do an initial check-in call as an introduction of themselves and their background, and to determine fit. This will give you a chance to talk to them about your goals and better understand their experience, and it allows for some personal discussion to assess likeability.

The other factor is fear of the unknown or a general misunderstanding of what coaching is. People confuse coaching with therapy or counseling, or they have a perception that it is fluffy. Business coaching is aligned on driving results through personal development of people. Coaching should align with the organization's goals and work individually with people to foster behavior change. Good coaches will challenge you to think differently, go further, and try new things. They will be your greatest advocate and your toughest critic while always having your best interests at heart. They will hold you accountable and allow you to dream big.

When I work with senior-level executives, what I hear most is that they appreciate the ability to talk about what is on their mind without judgment. I help them sort through their ideas and think of new ones. Senior people are often left to figure everything out themselves, and this can be unproductive as well as stressful. We all want to continue to improve and get better at what we do, and coaching can help.

11

Confidentiality in Coaching

IN EVERY COACHING INTERACTION, it is critical that the coachee feels comfortable that anything that is shared is kept confidential. It is important for any breakthroughs that the individual is able to truly share what is happening so that we as coaches can get to the root cause of any situation. If you are a manager having coaching conversations, you first need to ensure that you have a strong trust base with your employees before coaching can ever be successful. If you do not have trust, then this is the first step for you to work on as a manager or leader. We do not need to share confidential information in order to be able to write objectives or share back to the organization what we are working on. Through objectives of the business, we can show progress without having to explain any details of how we are getting there. Once employees open up and share what may be hindering their progress, we can then truly help define a different course of action for them to be successful. It is therefore critical that they feel that they can be open and honest with their coach.

12

Types of Coaching: Face-to-Face and Virtual

Face-to-Face Coaching

MOST OF US THINK that for coaching to be effective, we must do it in person. As a start, when you are first meet the person you will be coaching, it is highly valuable to unite in person and establish a connection. However, as you move through your coaching journey, you may not always be physically present to meet. It is still highly important to continue the coaching relationship even if you are not meeting in person.

Virtual Coaching

This form of coaching does not take place in person. It includes phone, webinar, or Skype. Phones are best for simple, new concepts or to follow up on previously discussed issues.

Webinars are best for large groups and can be used to present concepts, but they are not for interactive discussion.

The Skype option works well for time-sensitive or delicate issues.

In your role, you may be faced with situations where you will need to coach virtually. Virtual coaching will provide you with:

- More versatile options to meet
- Increased touch points.
- Flexibility, reduced travel time, and the ability to use your time efficiently
- Ways to address ad-hoc issues more quickly
- Greater collaborations through ongoing, interactive discussions
- Support and accountability to help sustain momentum
- A chance to listen and hear differently than over the phone, providing new insights

- Virtual coaching is ideal anytime your physical location doesn't make an in-person meeting possible.
- It is great when your schedules don't align or when you need to use your time more efficiently.
- You can use virtual coaching to address specific issues more quickly and to touch base with coachees in the moment.
- If you need to collaborate with a group, an interactive group coaching session can encourage good collaboration.
- If you're stuck or looking for a new way to approach a topic, try virtual coaching to take advantage of a different way of interacting.

  - It provides an opportunity to allow the coach to listen for tone of voice and other subtle nuances, without body language. It can be a more intimate experience because sometimes people are more comfortable opening up when you are not face-to-face. This makes it a great option if you are stuck or looking for a new way to approach a topic. In fact, research has even shown that gaze aversion can improve cognitive performance.

- Virtual coaching is any form of coaching that takes place through a channel other than face-to-face— usually by phone, webinar, webcam, or e-mail. It is simply using a form of technology to enable a coaching session when the coach and coachee are unable to meet in person.

- Besides the medium, there really isn't a major difference between virtual and face-to-face coaching. Coaching is coaching, regardless of how it happens.

- In fact, research on the topic has found that there is no difference in the reported level of problem resolution for face-to-face and virtual coaching sessions, and that both versions of coaching produced strong working alliances.

- As a coach, it is your job to create a safe and comfortable environment where you can ask good questions and dive into goals and strategies. A good coach will encourage coachees to do most of the talking, encouraging them to discover their own ideas, draw their own conclusions, and carve their own paths. These best practices are the same both in person or at a distance, however in a virtual session they are more likely to slip.

- This is why it's very important to respect the process by treating your virtual coaching sessions with the same importance as any other: preparing thoroughly, engaging fully, and encouraging the same from your coachees.

- The **phone** is best for simple, new concepts or to follow up on previously discussed issues. It's also great for quick, ad-hoc touch points.

- **Webinars** are best for large groups. They can be used to present concepts but not to have good interactive discussion. If you require data or facts in your session, using a visual (like a WebEx) may better allow your coachees to process your information.
- The webcam works well for time-sensitive or delicate issues.
- One tool for virtual coaching you will likely use often is Skype for Business. It is very useful both for one-on-one and group coaching session, and you can easily have phone calls or do video conferencing, including desktop sharing. It even supports collaboration on Microsoft Office documents, which makes working together on shared documents such as an action plan fairly smooth.

There are some drawbacks to virtual coaching, which you can often mitigate.

- You don't get the same ability to read body language, facial expressions, and gestures in virtual settings. As a coach, you also lose the opportunity to show your engagement and focus through your body language.
- Managing the scheduling of a virtual coaching session can be challenging, especially if you're dealing with time zone differences or coachees who spend most of their time on the road.
- You're more likely to encounter issues with technology during a virtual session—Wi-Fi connection issues, quality of audio, frozen screens. We'll discuss what to do to avoid these problems later in this module.
- It takes practice to be able to collaborate smoothly when virtually interacting with a person. Working together to complete an action plan or to review a document can be challenging, but it can work well as long as you prepare for it.

My Favorite Simple Coaching Framework

Introduction of the Four Steps of the Coaching Framework

Using a four-step approach will help you to become more comfortable with a coaching approach. We always prepare ahead of time before any sessions to ensure that we have any data or facts that may help us through the conversation. As managers, we also may have our own objectives for the coaching session. What is most important is to remember that coaching is always about the coachees and meeting them where they are at. Guiding them to our objective will not allow for getting to the root cause of any situation, and therefore there will no real change. By following these four phases, you will have a step-by-step approach to ensuring a successful coaching conversation. The first step is to let go of anything that is on your mind and be in the moment; be focused on your coachees and what is happening in their world.

Coaching Conversation Framework

Step One: Open

Prepare for the conversation. Refer back to your last session, review any and all key points, and focus on the action plan items and key takeaways.

Create a coaching strategy; plan with three to five questions prepared (use of powerful questions).

Before the session begins, take five minutes to focus your mind on being present in the moment. Remove all barriers and thoughts that may be consuming you, and try to focus in on the person.

Create a warm and engaging space for your employees when they enter the room.

Have some opening dialogue to set them at ease.

Start with a question on focusing the conversation on the topic you would like to address, or ask them what they would like to talk about today.

Introduce the coaching agreement process.

Use powerful questions and probing techniques to draw out the insights and allow for self-discovery.

The goal is to continue to probe until you feel like you have found the root cause of the behavior or problem.

Once they have an aha moment or specific tangibles are determined, then you can move to the next phase.

Step Two: **Discover**

In this phase, you ask questions to start addressing the key areas identified in the discovery phase.

We want people to feel free to brainstorm new ideas and generate creative options here.

Be open and flexible to new ideas and new ways of approaching situations.

Allow for self-exploring of topics or next steps.

Step Three: Create

In this phase, you start to create solid next steps around a how-to solution for the areas identified.

What are the key things that need to happen?

Who needs to help and be involved in the plan?

What specific steps need to occur for success?

Step Four: Action

In this phase, you set two to three specific action items with timelines and accountability measures.

If it is your first session, fill in the details on the coaching agreement, as well as ensure an action plan is completed.

These are documented in their individual coaching plans that are kept on file for performance-measurement purposes.

The coach helps to keep the person accountable for these measures and keeps a score on accountability, to be calculated at the end of the year.

The outcome or success of the initiative also needs to be rank scored because it relates back to the company's KPI metrics.

The Coaching Framework

1. Open	2. Discover
In this phase, you set the stage for an effective coaching conversation.	*In this phase, you learn more about the coachee's perspective and help him or her to start thinking of what could be.*
<ul><li>Assess what the coachee would like to cover</li><li>Define specific desired outcome for coaching session</li><li>Outline the coaching agreement</li><li>Open with questions that will make the person feel comfortable while building trust</li></ul>	<ul><li>Engage in building an environment of trust, respect, and open dialogue</li><li>Ask open-ended questions to ensure clarity and understanding while gaining the coachee's perspective</li><li>Utilize observation and listening skills to determine the root cause of the situation one wants coaching on</li><li>Allow for brainstorming of many ideas</li></ul>
3. Create	4. Action
In this phase, you start to create solid ideas and the next steps to address the areas identified.	*In this phase, you ensure clarity on what you and your coachee are accountable for.*
<ul><li>Facilitate a discussion where the coachee generates solutions aligned with business and or personal priorities</li><li>Manage the coaching dialogue to gain agreement on solution and implementation</li><li>Collaborate with the coachee to create an action plan</li></ul>	<ul><li>Create a clear expectation for the action plan, evaluation criteria, and related positive outcomes or negative consequences</li><li>Leverage the coachee's strengths and development opportunities by monitoring progress from coaching session to session</li><li>Measure achievement of identified goals</li><li>Actively seek out feedback with a positive intent to strengthen coaching behaviour and coaching culture</li></ul>

13

How to Coach to Address Performance Situations

As YOU PREPARE FOR your coaching session, you should consider where the employee falls in regard to areas of focus. Is a particular issue with either skill, will, or hill, which will help you determine the root causes of a coachee's particular performance situation? Does the performance issue result from a lack of knowledge (skill) in a particular area, a lack of motivation (will) to achieve success, or obstacles present in the work environment (hill)?

Ask yourself the following questions to explore the three potential root causes of performance situations.

Ability	Motivation	Obstacle
• Does the person have the knowledge or skill to complete the goal? • Has this been done before and performed well?	• Is the person motivated to accomplish this goal? • What is the person's confidence level in regard to this goal?	• Is there an organizational or external environmental dynamic that is preventing the person from achieving the goal?

By assessing the coachee's commitment to change (high/low) and skill (high/low), you can determine the hypothesis of the coachee's behaviours (know/care), which will tell you which coaching quadrant you should use for your preparation.

Ability Assessment	Hypothesis of the Coachee's Behaviours	Situational Coaching Technique
High skill, high will	Know, care	Motivate
Low skill, high will	Care, don't know	Teach
High skill, low will	Know, don't care	More Directive
Low skill, low will	Don't know, don't care	Performance Plan

It's also important to frequently assess the coachee's ability commitment to change throughout the coaching process. Navigate to the appropriate coaching technique when a change occurs. Remember to approach all coaching situations with an open mind and free from any judgment. Knowing your coaching technique can help you prepare for your conversation, but it shouldn't define the coachee. An individual's level of motivation and skill is fluid, so be prepared to change your approach in the moment as you see fit.

14

Powerful Questions

What Are These, and How Do We Use Them in Coaching?

POWERFUL QUESTIONS CREATE GREATER awareness and clarity, and they invite people to action and discovery. These questions are generally open-ended, effective, solutions-focused, and reflective. They provide an individual with opportunities to tap into thoughts, feelings, and ideas they may not have realized they had, and they can self-discover their own solutions to problems.

Coaches use questions as their tool kit. The better you are at asking strategic, thought-provoking questions that allow the coachee to self-discover, the better coach you will become. It is always best to come prepared with your top ten questions ready to go so you can pull them up whenever you need them.

Open-ended questions encourage coachees to open up and reveal more information, both to you and to themselves. They help coachees to consider new possibilities, explore their own thoughts and feelings, and self-discover their own solutions for moving forward. You should aim to ask open-ended questions that create greater possibility for:

- Anticipation
- Assessment
- Clarification
- Elaboration
- Expanded learning
- Fresh perspective

In Michael Bungay Stanier's book *The Coaching Habit*, he offers "Seven Good Questions" that can radically improve your coaching conversations. Consider the following questions and the effect they could have with your coaches.

1. Kickstart Question—"What's on your mind"
   This question gets to the heart of the matter fast.

2. The Awe Question—"And what else?"
   Possibly the best coaching question, because a their first answer is rarely their only answer or their best answer.

3. The Focus Question—"What is the real challenge here for you?"
   This question gets to the bottom of the problem, and it turns the focus to solving the real problem, not just the first problem.

4. The Foundation Question—"What do you want?"
   This question gets you deeper into the conversation and can be particularly helpful if negative emotions may have derailed the focus of the conversation.

5. The Lazy Question—"How can I Help?"
   This question forces the coachee to make a clear request

for what you can do, without stepping in and taking away the coachee's ownership of the solution.

6. The Strategic Question—"If you are saying yes to this, what are you saying no to?"
   This is a great question for someone who says yes to every request. It forces coachees to identify their boundaries so they don't become overwhelmed and overcommitted.

7. The Learning Question—"What was most useful for you?"
   This question is your closer, and it helps finish your conversation on a strong note. It has the coachee identify value on the conversation and reinforces learning.

The following table presents some guidelines when asking powerful questions.

Do	Don't
• Ask questions that start with "what" and "how," increasing the odds that your questions will be nonleading	• Don't ask questions that start with "Did you," "Have you," or "Do you" (which will lead to your solution)
• Ask questions that engage the coachees in seeing their situation differently	• Don't ask questions that gather facts that *you* are curious about (which don't add insight for the coachee)
• Ask questions that focus on the coachees' role in the situation and what is within their control and influence	• Don't ask questions so that *you* can fully understand all of the details of the situation
• Keep track of questions that consistently work well for you; build a repertoire of powerful questions	• Don't ask "why" questions, which tend to put people on the defensive; turn them into "what" questions instead.

As you gain more experience as a coach, you will develop a repertoire of powerful questions that you will draw on as the moment calls for it See the appendix for an extensive list of sample Powerful Questions.

Using Powerful Questions as a Tool

Asking questions isn't just about the answer. Powerful questions often give individuals the opportunity to frame their situation differently or approach it from a different perspective. The answers to the questions aren't for the coach; they are to help coachees move forward and find their own solutions.

Asking powerful questions encourages people to think deeply and reflect on their situation. Reflection is important because it is during this time that the brain makes new connections. Research indicates that the human brain produces alpha waves during reflection, a brain state associated with relaxed awareness, and that we are thinking in a way that allows our unconscious brain to think. This allows those connections to be made across the whole brain, not just with those areas that we are consciously thinking about. Thus, powerful questions can create more self-awareness and open the mind up to various new possibilities.

By being in the moment with your coachee, using listening skills, and trusting in your ability to ask powerful questions, you will set yourself up for successful coaching conversations.

Great coaches utilize powerful questions to expand the thinking and decision-making effectiveness of those they coach. Remember that our goal in coaching is to guide the conversation so that coachees identify their own best solution and next steps. The coachees will learn more in the process because they are doing more of the heavy lifting. Review the table on the following page to consider the types of questions you might ask.

Coaching Questions for Discover

The following are just a few examples of the types of questions you might ask during the discovery phase. They help you to open up the conversation to help the coachee identify the root of the issue and to see it (and potential solutions) from various perspectives. The goal is to explore deeply the issue the coachees have identified and to ask question that allow them to create connections and consider thoughts, feelings, and ideas they otherwise might not have. See the appendix for a more comprehensive list of questions.

Discover
What do you want to achieve?
By the end of the conversation, what would you like to accomplish?
What is most important to you right now?
How do you see this situation?
What is happening?
What is working?
What is not working?
What makes this challenging?
What is stopping you?
How might others describe the situation?
What is the experience you are looking to create?
What impact is this having on you? On others?
What are the consequences if the situation doesn't change?
How does this influence your goals and what you want to accomplish?
What are the long-term implications?

Evaluating Options

During the discover phase, you will have encouraged your coachees to generate a number of options for possible solutions to their situation. It is during the create phase that you will review and evaluate these options together. Consider the following when evaluating the options.

- Which will have the greatest impact on the business?

- How much time, money, and resources will be required?
- How are the coachees leveraging their strengths?
- Which is most aligned with personal, team, and company goals?
- What will be required of the coach?

Coaching Questions for Create

- The following are just a few examples of the types of questions you might ask during the Create phase. They help guide the coachees to consider and evaluate various solutions to their problems and rely on themselves to establish next steps. See the appendix for a more comprehensive list of questions.

Create
What could you do?
What have you tried?
What would work?
What might be some approaches to take?
What else might work?
What major barriers are preventing this change from happening?
Where would the biggest resistance from that change come from? What will you do?
When will you do it?
What specific actions will help you achieve your goal?
What will your first steps be? When will you start?
Who can help hold you accountable?
How will you stay focused?
How can I support you?
When can we follow up?

15

Bias and Perception Check

WHEN PREPARING FOR A coaching session, the coach analyzes data, looking for performance and behaviour indicators (or symptoms) and the outcomes associated with them. It's very important to check for your own bias when you have analyzed the data. Remember that being free from judgment is one of the coaching competencies.

Ask yourself the following questions to see whether you have bias or perception traps.

- "Do I have a bias/perception of this person?" We tend to view others holistically—all good (the halo effect) or all bad (the pitchfork effect)—and rate those similar to ourselves as higher (the "similar to me" effect).
- How closely do my thoughts mirror the data, outcomes, and documentation?
- How rigorously have I checked my perceptions for accuracy or compared them to the standards?
- How do I ensure that the coachees—or even I as the coach—doesn't have a "perceived" versus "real" obstacle in their way?

Looking at the data, the person, and the situation in this way helps to remove biases by raising our own awareness. It's a way to challenge our own thinking!

Ability/Motivation/Obstacle

When preparing for a coaching conversation, it is important to remember that people are on their own journeys of development. Once you've completed the bias and perception check, this is where you begin the assessment, which can help you to determine the root cause of a coachee's particular performance situation. Is it a skill issue? If so, maybe people require more training? If it is a motivational issue, then what is causing this, and how can you ask the right questions to pull this out? If it is an organizational situation, then determining what control your coachees may have or not and helping them manage it may be the key to helping them move in a different direction. Remember that there does not always need to be any of these barriers in place; you may have a motivated skilled employee looking for different kinds of support.

Based on the root cause, adjust your previous analysis and reexamine the performance documentation. Once again, check yourself: "Am I applying any bias?" Once you have determined where your coachee is within the three areas to focus for coaching, remember that no situation is static. You should reassess the situation regularly during your coaching process, adjusting your approach and your coachee's situation evolves.

16

Creating a Coaching Agreement

ONE OF THE MOST important steps in any coaching conversation is to start with an agreement of what you will cover, how you will work together, and specific objectives to work toward. When you are in a more formal executive coaching situation, a coaching agreement is signed during the first session. This allows people to feel comfortable about the confidentiality piece, it also helps to align on when and where you will meet, and it holds accountability to the process. In a corporate environment, it is still important to use either a coaching agreement or an action planning process to ensure that there is documentation regarding what you agree on for next steps.

Here is an example of a basic coaching agreement.

Name of Coach:
Name of Coachee:
Date of First Session:

Time, Place, and Frequency of Coaching:
Three monthly sessions or coaching during

regular one-on-one with manager. Be as specific as possible to ensure a strong commitment.

Confidentiality: This paragraph should align with the ICF definition of coaching confidentiality.

Objectives of Coaching Sessions: This is where you align on the topics and objectives that you would like to work on, as well as any specific timelines against those objectives

Agree on the Next Steps: List any specific next steps from your first session, and then an action plan should be created for each additional session. Ensure these are SMART goals and that these are reviewed and aligned with both the coach and the coachee.

Signature of Coach:
Signature of Coachee:

When organizations pay for executive or corporate coaching, they may ask for a copy of this agreement to show that the goals of the coaching align with the corporation goals. This is what we call a sponsor in coaching. To ensure confidentiality, these can be written more generally to show trends and overall concepts. The action plans would then need to be more specific for the coachee to follow and would provide more individual areas of focus.

17

Your Coaching Approach

PLANNING AHEAD WILL HELP you determine your approach to coaching. These elements may also focus your approach even more.

- Both the coach's and coachee's strengths
- Your history and relationship with the coachee
- The status of the coachee's short- and long-term business goals
- The coachee's development goals and career aspirations
- The coachee's interests
- Your knowledge of resources to support the coachee

It pays to review the coachee's strengths to make your coaching approach the most effective it can be. Recall the strengths-based approach to coaching. A strengths-based approach to coaching leverages a coachee's strengths to better position the person for success. For example, someone who is analytical would appreciate reviewing data. Someone who is very focused would benefit from just one to two focus areas at a time. Remember too that sometimes your own strengths and social style can clash with those of your coachee. It's important to check any bias and consider approaching the conversation differently so that you can both thrive.

Your history and relationship with the coachee can also influence how the conversation can go. If you have a good working relationship with the coachee, you will have an easier time getting the person to open up. If you don't know each other well or have had any tension in your history, you should spend more time building that needed trust and rapport.

Tailoring your approach to consider your coachee's development goals, career aspirations, and interests will also help you have a successful conversation. Your coachee's goals, aspirations, and interests are likely the ones he or she is most motivated by and knowledgeable in, which will go far in engaging the coachee and adding depth to the conversation.

The resources you have available to support the coachee will help determine what your coachee is able to do to solve problems and manage situations. If you know there are lots of resources available, you can encourage your coachee to think bigger and to consider more options for solutions to the situation. If you don't have many resources available, you'll need to encourage your coachee to think more creatively in order to work with the resources you already have.

Overall, you have put a lot of work into preparing for your coaching conversation, but it is essential that you not allow any of the information you've gathered to bias your perspective. You must always approach each coaching conversation free from judgment. As you enter the next phase, feel prepared, but use that preparedness to allow you to truly be in the moment. Trust that your preparations will help your conversation to be smooth and informed, but approach the conversation completely open, as if everything you will learn today will be new.

18

Building Trust

TRUST IS THE FOUNDATION of coaching and looks different to everyone. It is essential to a coaching relationship. For coachees, it takes a great deal of trust to be able to fully open up and explore their deep thoughts and feelings with another person. They must be comfortable with the confidentiality agreement, trusting that their coach will maintain a very high degree of confidentiality. On the other side, the coach needs to trust that the coachees are serious about the coaching relationship and will do the work necessary to be successful.

Building trust comes down to a few key things: credibility, reliability, and intimacy.

Credibility refers to the things you say as a coach. If you say things that are believable and sincere, you build credibility.

Reliability refers to your actions as a coach. If others can depend on you to deliver on what you promise, you become reliable.

Intimacy is about the feelings of safety and security that you give others when they entrust you with something. By respecting others' confidentiality and respecting their personal thoughts and feelings, you create intimacy.

Self-orientation refers to individuals' focus on themselves. If you are focused on yourself, you communicate that you don't care much about the other person, or that you're not paying attention.

Credibility, reliability, and intimacy are the basis of trust, and the more you exhibit these traits, the more trustworthy you become. Being focused on others is a coaching skill, and so the more self-oriented you are, the less trustworthy you are to others.

Sometimes building the kind of trust to have an open and transparent coaching conversation takes time. Remember everyone's style is different, so don't worry if things don't seem smooth the first time. Continuing to reinforce your good intentions and asking for feedback will go a long way in building those bridges. If it doesn't seem to be working, ask coachees if the fit is working for them; if possible, a coach chemistry change may be needed. If you are their manager, it is crucial you work through these trust barriers.

19

Listening Skills

To HAVE AN ENGAGED coachee, we have to model active engagement. We do this with a listening technique called level three listening.

When you are not being listened to, you:	Level Three Listening:
• Feel disrespected	• Gains respect
• Lose engagement	• Builds relationship and trust
• Lose rapport	• Creates open communication

Level three listening is a very powerful form of listening that allows you to connect more closely with other people in a conversation and better understand their needs. This is different from active listening in that it involves a deeper understanding of what's being communicated. To get a better understanding of level three listening, you need to be familiar with the three levels of listening.

Level one listening is all about me. It involves focusing on ourselves and noticing what's going on inside our heads during a conversation. We might hear what other people are saying, but we're relating their words to our own experiences, opinions, and feelings: "What should I say next?" Level one listeners are not giving the speaker their full attention because they are distracted by thinking of their own experiences and connecting the conversation to those experiences. Distractions might even include unrelated thoughts, such as what you might eat for lunch.

Level two listening is all about the other person. It involves focusing intently on the speaker, listening carefully to what is being said. You give the speaker your full attention, ignoring the distractions of your inner dialogue and the environment around you. Even when you are speaking during a level two conversation, you are still focused on the other person, summarizing what is said and asking questions to probe deeper. Despite the strong level of focus in level two listening, you are still missing some of the deeper meaning in the conversation. This is where level three listening comes into play.

Level three listening still focuses on the other person, but it involves listening to the *environment* of the person and the conversation, in addition to the words spoken. It requires you to take in what's happening in the space around you but without allowing it to distract you. You read the vibe and energy of the conversation, picking up on elements like body language, gestures, emotions, mood, inflections, tone, and pace. (Is there tension between us? Is our conversation flat or full of energy? What *isn't* being said?) Level three listening also entails understanding how the energy of the environment affects your interaction and then adapting yourself accordingly. This will add meaning and depth to your conversation, allowing you to connect more closely with your speaking partner.

Level three listening is a difficult skill that requires practice and discipline. There are many components involved in being an effective level three listener, but they can be narrowed down to the following.

- Being present
- Demonstrating empathy
- Asking thoughtful questions
- Eliminating judgment
- Reading the situation

To truly engage in level three listening, you need to practice using all of these elements together. It's the combination of them that will elevate your listening skills to the highest level.

Being present is a state of awareness that lets you fully attend to what is happening in the moment. It is itself a skill that takes practice, but it becomes easier with time. To practice being present, you need to ensure you have enough time to have your conversation. If you are pressed for time, you won't be able to let go of these concerns, which will distract you. You also need to start with a positive mindset because any frustration, anger, or stress can divert your attention away from the conversation and back to yourself. Make sure you stop everything else you're doing besides listening; put away your phone, computer, or anything else that could occupy your attention. Focus fully on the person in front of you and resist diverting your attention to distractions. When distractions do come up (and they will), recognize that they are there but allow them to pass without focusing on them. To be present, try to slow down. Don't worry about what to say next or filling any silences. Quiet the chatter in your head and allow yourself to become fully engaged in the conversation.

Demonstrating empathy for speakers can encourage them to express themselves more freely. To practice and demonstrate empathy, try to read the emotions behind speakers' words. Notice their tone, pacing, and intonation. Observe their facial expressions and body language for signs of emotions, such as excitement, frustration, defeat, or stress. When you hear or observe an emotion, acknowledge it: "It sounds like that makes you angry." "Sounds like you're feeling discouraged." You can also demonstrate empathy through your behavior and body language. Be attentive and show interest in the speaker, listening carefully while ignoring all distractions. Maintain an open and relaxed posture, make eye contact, and match your facial expression with the speaker's.

Asking thoughtful questions can help you elicit deeper and more meaningful information from your speaker, plus show that you're interested and paying attention. Try to ask open-ended questionsbecause they will encourage speakers to open up to you and explore their ideas more fully. For example, "Can you tell me more about that?" "What might happen if you …?" When asking questions, focus on quality over quantity. Too many questions can make people feel like they are being interrogated, which can make them close down. Instead, keep your questions limited to only meaningful and relevant ones; this will show that you understand and are interested. When speakers answer a question, try pausing for a few seconds to allow them the opportunity to continue their thoughts instead of jumping in with further questions or comments.

Eliminating judgment from your environment will help people speak more openly and will make you more receptive to their message. We all judge, even subconsciously, and so it takes practice to eliminate judgment from an interaction. When conversing with others, try to let go of any preconceived notions and be open to what they have to say. Aim to understand rather than evaluate or criticize. Accept people as they are and respect their points of view. This will make you better able to understand what is said, and it reduces distractions from within. Use body language and behavior to create a safe and comfortable environment. Show that you are interested and genuine by using open posture, making eye contact, and nodding occasionally. Avoid interrupting the speaker or injecting your own thoughts or suggestions. Even if you don't necessarily agree with speakers, validate their feelings and perspective to show that you understand. Make sure not to minimize or trivialize any of their concerns.

Reading the situation involves allowing the emotion and energy in the conversation to inform your understanding. Notice the energy between you and the speaker, and how it shifts throughout your interaction. Is the conversation flat or enthusiastic? Do you sense frustration or interest? Be aware of other people's moods and attitudes and how they change as the conversation moves forward. Beyond what is being said, listen to *how* it is said. The tone, pacing, volume, and intonation of a person's voice can reveal a lot of information. Be observant of speakers' behaviours and body language. Do they seem relaxed, tense, interested, or distracted? Are they sitting on the edge of their chair? Is their desk a mess? Are they glancing occasionally at their computer screen, clock, or door? If they appear stressed, distracted, or frustrated, ask if there's a better time for them, ask about their concerns, and see if there's anything you can do to provide relief. When you feel you have a read on a situation, adjust your behavior and the conversation accordingly. If you sense negative energy or emotions, note what causes this and try a different approach. If you're reading interest or enthusiasm, encourage the conversation to continue down this path.

20

Action Planning: Define Specific Outcomes of Coaching Session

Now that you and your coachee have generated and evaluated options for possible solutions to their situation, you need to help your coachee define specific outcomes of coaching session. This is where you can ask questions about what coachees will do, how they will begin, how they will monitor progress, and more. Their answers to these questions will represent the outcomes from your coaching session and will form the basis of your action plan.

Internal and External Considerations

It is necessary to consider logistics when coming up with actions your coachee will move forward on. Discuss these topics with your coachee when determining your next steps.

- Will the coachee require support from colleagues?
- Is there an adequate number of employees to support?
- Are there sufficient resources to accomplish these goals?
- Is there a budget that needs to be considered?

- Is the solution aligned with business goals?
- How will the success of the solution be determined?

Action Plan Process for Coaching

Creating an action plan with your coachee is an important part in exploring action. Ask your coachee questions about the following topics and note them in the Action Planning Worksheet.

- Goal setting with specific and measurable goals—SMART
- Possible subgoals
- Action steps
- Timeline (key milestones)
- Self-assessment checks
- Rewards and consequences

Action Plan Worksheet

Use the Action Plan Worksheet on the next page to help you establish next steps with your coachee. It will help you put the coachee's goals and next steps all into one place to help you both monitor progress. See below for details on how to make good use of the Action Plan Worksheet.

Coaching Action Plan

Name: **Coach:**
Next Coaching Session:

Action Plan Item	Details	Date
1. Ask Not Tell	-> Keep questions tight, and to the point, while genuine -> Shorter questions can deliver smoother flow, and result in timelier awareness	-> Jan 30: Immediate focus thru next 2-rounds of field days & coaching moments Next Coaching session
2. Focus on Competencies	-> Focus on being in the moment -> Ensure to remember what went well as well as opportunity's	-> On-going: Continue to recognize wins -> Jan 30: Immediate focus thru next 2-rounds of field days & coaching moments
3.Use powerful questions	-> Come prepared with 3 to 5 powerful questions -Practice them at every coaching session	-> Nov 30: Immediate action & exercised on all Field Days / Coaching Opportunities

What Does It Mean to Be Accountable?

Accountability is a personal choice to rise above one's circumstances and demonstrate the ownership necessary for achieving key results—to see it, own it, solve it, and do it.

The accountability phase is built in action, adding clear and measurable expectations for what is going to happen. This means specific timelines, with due dates and metrics that can indicate how the plan is going and when it is complete.

Coach and Coachee Accountability

In general, the coachee owns the commitments from coaching. However, the coach is also accountable for a number of elements.

- The coach ensures the process of coaching follows the coaching model
- The coach ensures coachees know what they are accountable for.
- How do you communicate expectations and measurement?
- The coach is also a leader and so is also accountable for results and for tasks of management: removing obstacles, providing resources, and aligning actions to plans and strategies.

21

Coaching for Performance

COACHING SPANS A CONTINUUM from "in the moment" on one end to "longer term and future oriented" on the other. As a result, there are different types of coaching. However, they all share a common support of engaging in meaningful dialogue, providing regular feedback, and driving continuous improvement.

Performance coaching is generally a shorter-term type of coaching. It lasts approximately three to twelve months and has a more immediate and tangible focus, usually on improving performance and outcomes. Performance coaching relies mostly on feedback and might even incorporate some elements of teaching or showing. Performance coaching is often used when we're in the counseling phase of the situational coaching quadrants, when performance has become an issue.

Coaching for performance helps your employees be the best that they can be by unlocking their potential to maximize their own performance so that they can deliver great results for the organization. It's not about evaluating an employee's current performance but is focused on enabling future performance.

Coaching for performance is based on the belief that every employee wants to perform highly and is able to do so. It involves viewing people in a much more positive and optimistic way than we are generally accustomed to, especially in situations with performance issues, and treating them this way as well. Approaching your coaching with this belief creates engagement that drives this performance.

The GROW model is a well-known coaching model for structuring a coaching conversation in order to maximize an individual's potential. It is an approach or a philosophy, rather than a set of tools, comprised of four steps.

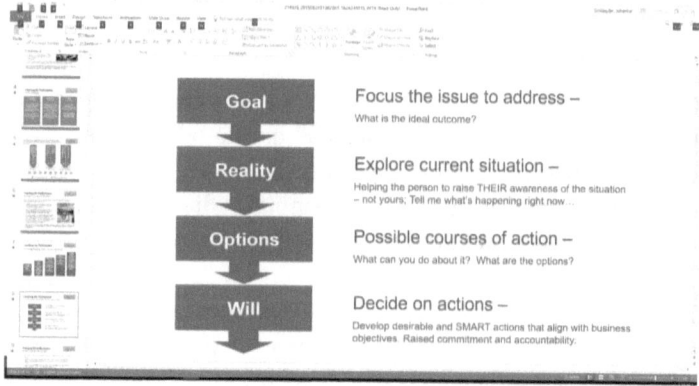

Your performance coaching conversation can start at any of the GROW stages. Perhaps your employees begin by telling you about an issue they are dealing with (reality), an action plan they're currently working through (will), something they want to accomplish (goal), or an idea they want to implement (options).

Goal: At some point in the conversation, it's important to establish at least one goal that the coachee wishes to accomplish, ideally one shorter-term goal for your coaching session and one longer-term performance goal. To encourage your coachee to define some goals. You may ask questions such as:

- What outcome would you like from this session?
- What would you like to happen that is not happening now?
- What do you want to achieve long term?

Reality: It is difficult to see any situation objectively, and so it's your job to help your coachees see their situation with as few biases and assumptions as possible. Asking them to describe their current situation helps you to explore the reality of the situation.

Options: Using a variety of questions to guide, help your coachee to identify as many different options for ideas and solutions to the situation as possible. Your job isn't to find the correct solution but to help the coachee explore what is possible.

Will: Use what you've discussed previously to help your coachees determine how they can achieve their goals. Use question to help your coachees evaluate their options and make a decision on a solution. Help your coachees take ownership over the solution by asking about the actions they will take, what obstacles might they run into, how they will manage these, and what resources they will need.

Coaching for Development

Contrary to coaching for performance, coaching for development has a longer-term focus. The goal is not only to deliver better outcomes but to learn through the process so that the learning and development can also apply to future tasks. Coaching for development is generally done when an employee is a high performer (skilled and motivated), and you are coaching in the motivating phase of the situational coaching quadrants. Here, your job is to support coachees in addressing their development needs that will bring them to the next level.

Coaching for development relies on good questions, helping participants to engage in their own reflection and discovery. With your coachees, you want to help them identify their strengths and establish a development plan. You will ask questions that encourage self-assessment, identify obstacles and ways around them, and evaluate a situation from a broader perspective. You will also help them establish the next steps that they will take to help their vision become a reality.

22

Coaching and Feedback

FEEDBACK IS AN ESSENTIAL element for developing people and improving performance. It's a useful tool for indicating when things are going in the right direction or for redirecting problem performance. Positive feedback reinforces behaviors that are working well, helping them to continue. Constructive or developmental feedback seeks to create a change in performance by providing specific information about particular individual behavior.

Giving and soliciting constructive feedback can be difficult because it takes courage and honesty to address performance gaps. Many individuals struggle with giving constructive feedback, but engaging in meaningful dialogue can help to develop an individual's performance and support our culture of continuous improvement.

When giving feedback, always begin by asking your coachee, "How are you doing?" or "How do you feel this went?" This is to help draw the feedback out; the coachees often already know how things are going, and your conversation can help them figure out your feedback themselves without needing to be explicitly told. If it doesn't work itself into the conversation or you need to provide more information, you can then ask if you can provide feedback. The following model provides ways to make your feedback constructive.

Coaching Approach Feedback Model

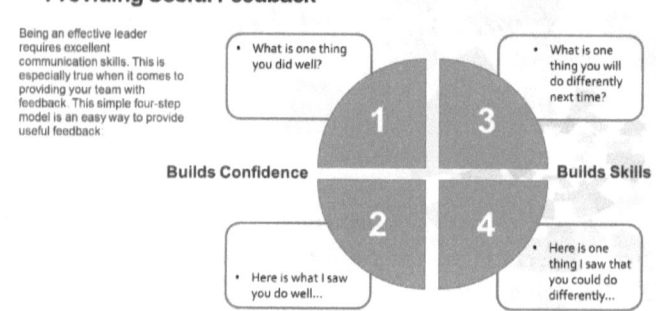

Providing Useful Feedback

Being an effective leader requires excellent communication skills. This is especially true when it comes to providing your team with feedback. This simple four-step model is an easy way to provide useful feedback

- What is one thing you did well?

- What is one thing you will do differently next time?

Builds Confidence

Builds Skills

- Here is what I saw you do well...

- Here is one thing I saw that you could do differently...

1   3
2   4

23

Using EQ and Other Assessments in Coaching

IT IS SOMETIMES OPTIMAL to have a tool to help you start a coaching conversation. It is the self-awareness of the coachee that is required in order to help set objectives and targets for development. If coachees do not think they need to be coached, then it is an uphill battle for the coach. Using assessments to identify areas of opportunity in performance can help to start off your coaching conversations at a more productive level. One of the assessments that works particularly well with leaders is the emotional intelligence indicator. The subtle nuances of EQ are sometimes the reasons we are held back in our careers. An EQ assessment can help to identify some of these areas.

Emotional intelligence (EQ) is the ability to be aware of our own emotions, as well as the emotions of others, and to leverage that information to better manage ourselves and our relationships. A strong EQ is a key element in strong coaching. Being able to identify and understand the emotions we feel in a coaching interaction helps us to avoid any influencing of our thoughts and feelings, which keeps us free from judgment and keeps us present in the moment.

By being able to pick up on the coachee's emotional state, we can better ask better questions to help dive into those feelings (or mitigate them) and generally manage the coaching relationship. We become skilled at picking up on what isn't being said in a conversation, which helps us to better understand and support the coachee's development.

Utilizing the EQ components from your own assessment and that of your coachee's can help you to use those insights to prepare for your coaching conversations and ensure that there is continuous progress in EQ skills. Being assertive and using your level three listening skills will help to ensure you are getting to the root cause so that the coaching conversation can be more successful. Remembering that you need to balance the components of empathy, emotional expression, and impulse control will help you to be a better coach.

Consider the following EQ coaching questions to add to your repertoire of questions.

EQ Coaching Questions

Empathy

- Tell me about a time when it was really important that you were able to understand the way someone else felt. How did you convey this understanding? How did you ensure you understood someone?
- Describe a situation where you were not as sensitive to someone's feelings as you should have been. Why do you think this was the case? What could you have done differently?
- In your opinion, what is the difference between sympathy and empathy? How do you ensure you display these differently?

- How do you ensure you have really understood how another person is feeling?
- Describe a situation where you found it difficult to make a decision because of the way the outcome might impact others. What was the result of your decision?

Emotional Expression

- Are there some emotions you feel more comfortable expressing than others? Why do you think that is? How do you express what you are feeling? Give examples.
- Describe a time when you regretted not having expressed your true thoughts or feelings about something. What were the consequences (positive and negative) of not expressing your feelings? How would the situation have been different had you been more expressive?
- In general, do you find yourself bottling up emotions? How does this affect your ability to get your work done?
- What does being happy look like to you? Being angry? Being frustrated?
- Have others ever misread your feelings or thoughts? Why do you think that happened?

Impulse Control

- How do you typically deal with an impulse to act?
- Tell me about a time when you had to exercise patience and control over your behavior.
- Describe a situation where you were impatient and reacted hastily. How did this impact the end result?
- Describe a situation where it was beneficial for you to act quickly. How did this make you feel?
- Has your impulsiveness ever created problems for you? How do you think others view your behavior in these instances?

24

Seven Easy Steps to Follow for a Successful Coaching Conversation

1. Coach Mode

Now that you are a coach, you need to be able to get your mindset into coach mode. Find something that helps you refocus from the day-to-day, quiet the mind, and eliminate the noise. As a leader, these moments may be needed quickly, so the more you practice, the better the focus will be on the employee versus on you. I sometimes say out loud "I am now going to put my coach hat on" because it reminds me and them that I am focused on them.

2. Prepare Questions in Advance

When you are preparing for a coaching session, pick your top three questions that you are most comfortable with and have them handy to use as needed. My favorite three are the following.

i. What else?
ii. What would happen if you didn't do that?
iii. How did that make you feel?

3. Create Solid Objectives

Creating objectives that are relevant and the coachee believes in are crucial for the coaching session to be successful and for future follow-through. Spend the time to craft these with the input of the coachee; fewer are better than too many.

4. Create a Solid Action Plan and Next Steps

This creates credibility for your session and brings closure to your meeting. It empowers the coachee and produces accountability for both of you.

5. Be Yourself

You always need to be genuine so that your coachee can be as well. People know when you are not being yourself, and this does not help to build trust or to have an open and transparent conversation. For some of us as leaders, this will be uncomfortable at first, but it will bring us the greatest benefit once we find our way.

6. If You Get Stuck, Take a Moment to Pause

Don't stress. Every new coach needs time to regroup or think about the next question. When in doubt, ask for feedback: Is this working for you? What do you want more or less of? What would help you most today?

7. Practice, Practice, Practice

Find a learning buddy whom you can trust to help you. Create scenarios of things you are dealing with. Role-play with your partner and ask for feedback. If you are comfortable, ask for a third person to observe and give feedback.

Remember

1. Listen deeply.
2. Questions are your greatest tool.
3. If you care about your people, it will show, so relax!

Appendix

Powerful Questions

THE FOLLOWING ARE QUESTIONS to help you in preparing for your coaching conversations. Some are best used ahead of time when you are planning your session, and some are good for in-the-moment practice. All are great questions to draw out the root cause of the issues by allowing self-discovery.

Powerful Questions 1.0

These are used for when you are stuck in the moment. Also, they are for you to try something new and go in a different direction if you are using the same questions all of the time.

- If I were to give you an extra hour a day, what would you do with it?
- What would you try now if you knew you could not fail?
- Just because that happened in the past, why must it happen again?
- If time is your currency, how would you spend it?
- If your money could talk, what would it say to you?
- What is the experience you are looking to create?

- How does this decision match up with who you know you are?
- When will you start?
- What small steps can you take to get you closer to your vision?
- What are you waiting for?
- What do you think the moral of that story is?
- What would you do if you had unlimited resources?
- What part of what you've just said could be an assumption?
- What are the positive outcomes of this negative situation?
- What story do you most often hear yourself telling?
- And …?
- If you knew the answer, what would it be?
- What am I not asking you that you really want me to ask?
- What story is holding you back?
- What will you do first?
- What's holding you back?
- How much energy are you willing to put into that?
- How would your ideal self create a solution?
- What are you trying to prove to yourself?
- If I was in your shoes and asked for advice, what would be the first thing you'd tell me?
- What have you tried that works well?
- How might you have contributed to this situation?
- How might others describe the situation?
- What are the consequences to you if this doesn't change?
- What is within your control or influence here?
- What does the ideal outcome look like?
- What are three different approaches you could take to reach that ideal state?
- What would work?
- How will you measure success?
- Where would the biggest resistance to this change come from?
- What will your first steps be? When will you start?

- How can I support you? When should we follow up and check progress?

Powerful Questions 2.0

Frame the Conversation
What is the most important thing for us to focus on?
How might I help you with this issue?
By the end of the conversation, what would you like to accomplish?
What else would you like to make sure we address?

Agree on the Process for the Conversation
Here's how I thought we could proceed ...
How does that sound?

Understand the Current State
How do you see this situation?
What is happening?
What is working well?
What makes this challenging?
How might you have contributed to this situation?
How might others see this situation?

Determine Consequences of Staying on Current Path
What impact is this having on you? On others?
What are the consequences if the situation doesn't change?
How does this influence your goals and what you are trying to accomplish?
What are the long-term implications?

Explore the Desired State
What would you like to see happen here?
What would the ideal state look like?
What are your goals? What would you like to accomplish?
What would success feel like? How would you know?

What might be some approaches to take?

What else might work?

What major barriers are preventing this change from happening?

Where would the biggest resistance from that change come from?

Lay Out a Success Plan

What specific actions will help you achieve your goal?

What will your first steps be? When will you start?

Who can help hold you accountable?

How will you stay focused?

How can I support you?

When should we touch base on this again?